THE STARS

A Gazillion Suns

LAURA PERDEW

Illustrated by Shululu

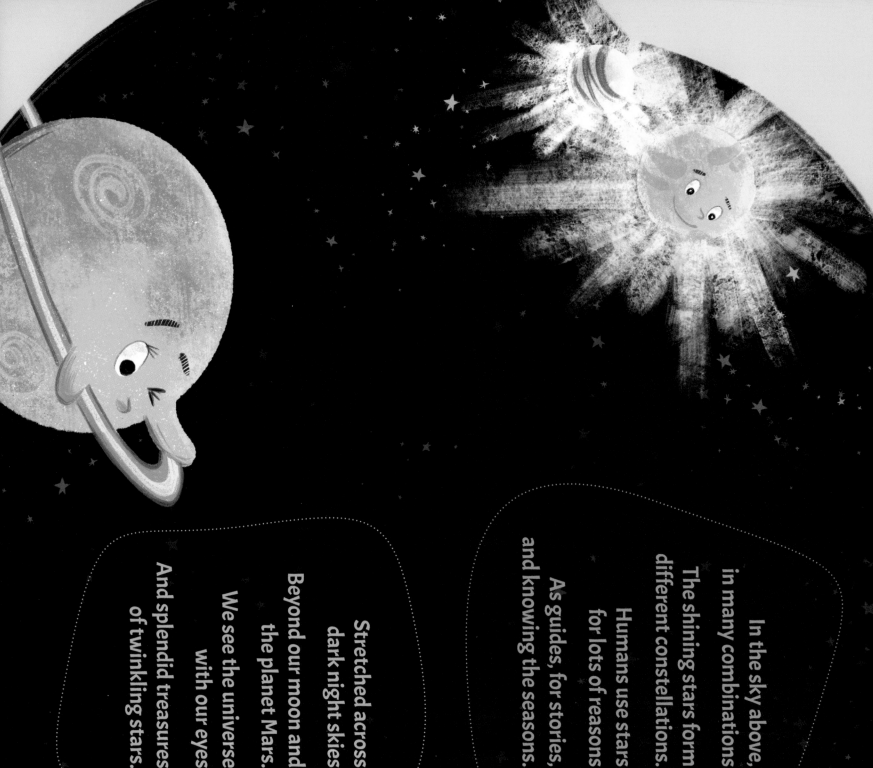

In the sky above,
in many combinations
The shining stars form
different constellations.

Humans use stars
for lots of reasons
As guides, for stories,
and knowing the seasons.

Stretched across
dark night skies
Beyond our moon and
the planet Mars.
We see the universe
with our eyes
And splendid treasures
of twinkling stars.

Hello, Earthlings!

Universe here. As you know, I am the amazing and vast expanse of space, full of planets and bright stars.

Do you know how many stars I have?

In fact, I have **WAAAAAAY** more stars than you can see. I have more than you can even count!

A LOT!

In the Milky Way alone—that's your galaxy—there are more than **100 billion stars!**

And I have more than

two million MILLION

galaxies.

Each one of them is a stage with

billions

of their own dazzling stars.

It's a galaxy older than 10 billion years, not a toy.

The Milky Way is pretty—it's shaped like a pinwheel.

Told you I have a lot of stars!

In your solar system, though, there is only one star—your sun.

It is the closest star to Earth. That's why it looks so much bigger than all the other stars. Those other stars you can see are light years away, so they seem very small to you.

Faraway stars look small,
but each one is
a massive,
SUPER-hot
ball of gas that makes
its own heat and light.

So their sun isn't such a hotshot star after all, is it?

Well, to them it is.

Some stars are smaller and cooler than your sun, and many are much larger and hotter than your sun.

Some of my largest stars are more than **a thousand times bigger** than your sun.

Yet they all start out the same—as a cloud of gas and dust. Then, with help from gravity, a star is born.

My remarkable baby stars are called protostars.

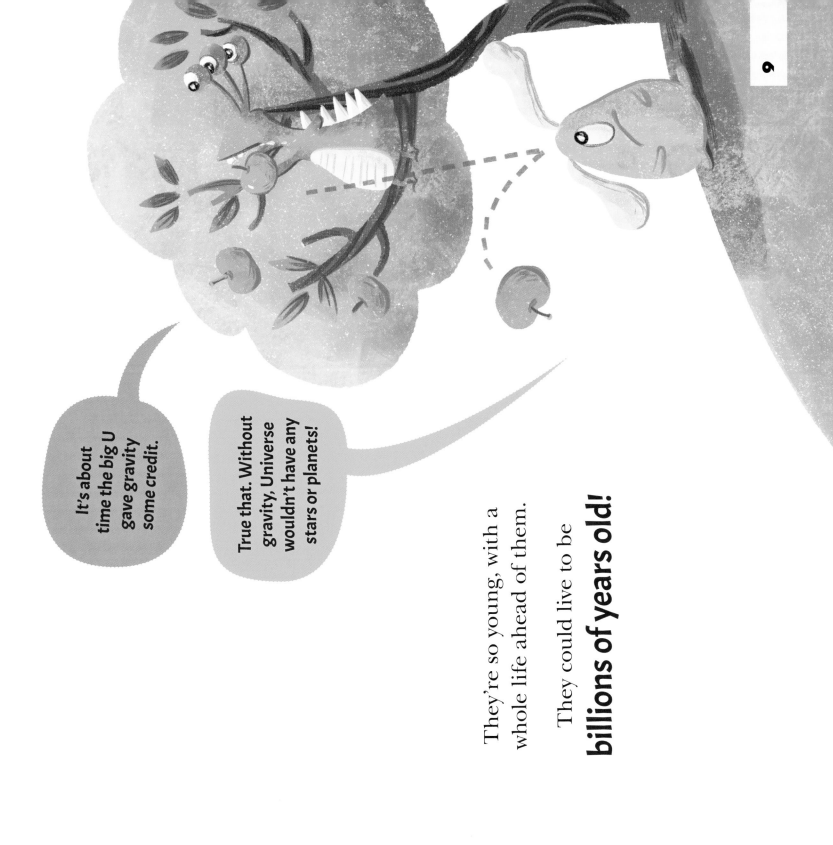

It's about time the big U gave gravity some credit.

True that. Without gravity, Universe wouldn't have any stars or planets!

They're so young, with a whole life ahead of them.

They could live to be **billions of years old!**

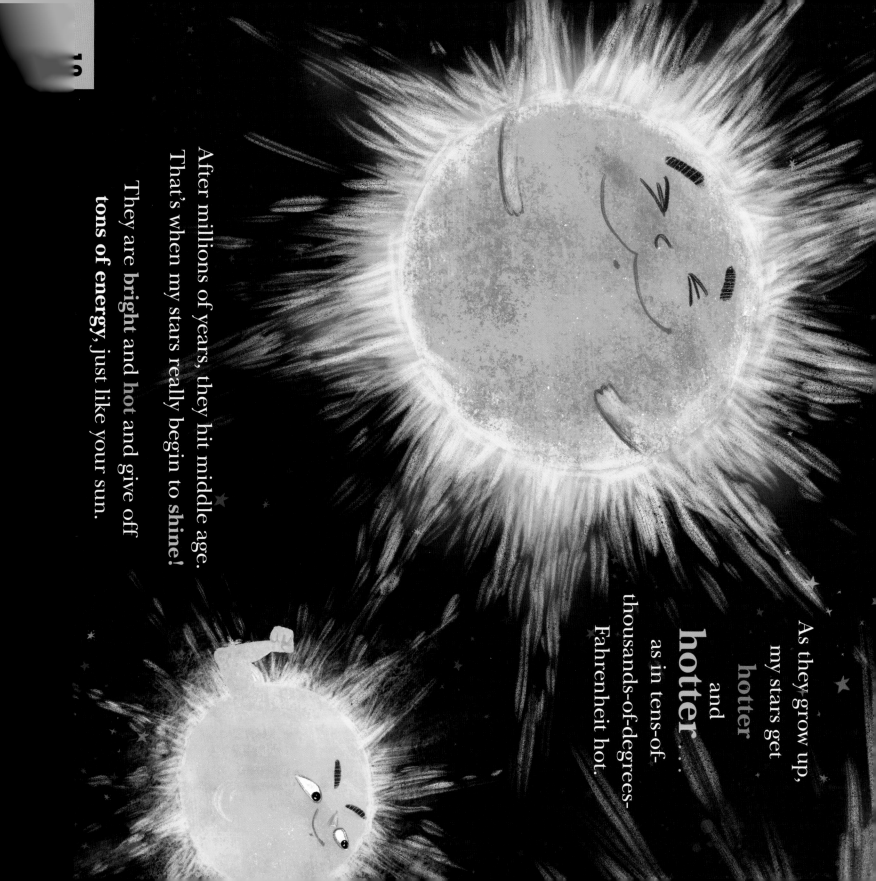

After millions of years, they hit middle age.
That's when my stars really begin to **shine**!

They are **bright** and **hot** and give off
tons of energy, just like your sun.

As they grow up,
my stars get
hotter
and
hotter . . .
as in tens-of-
thousands-of-degrees-
Fahrenheit hot.

And different colors, too—blue, orange, red, or white!

Some are bigger than others. Some are brighter.

They're not all like Earth's sun.

Speaking of your sun,
you've probably noticed
that you have only one.

It is a solitary star.

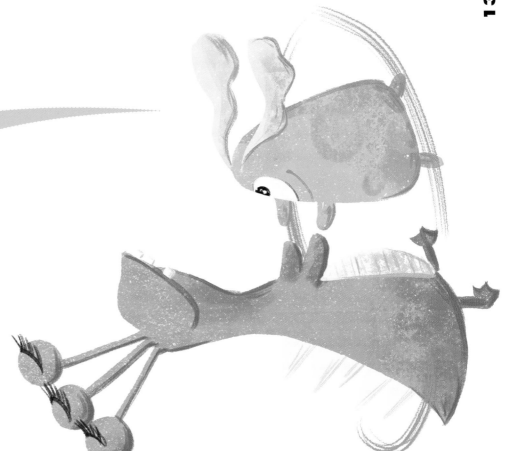

Maybe. It doesn't have another star to dance with as some stars do.

I wonder if Earth's sun gets lonely.

It doesn't have a star buddy.

But many of my other stars are twins! **Or triplets!**

Those stars stick together and circle one another.

Can you imagine life on Earth if you had two suns?

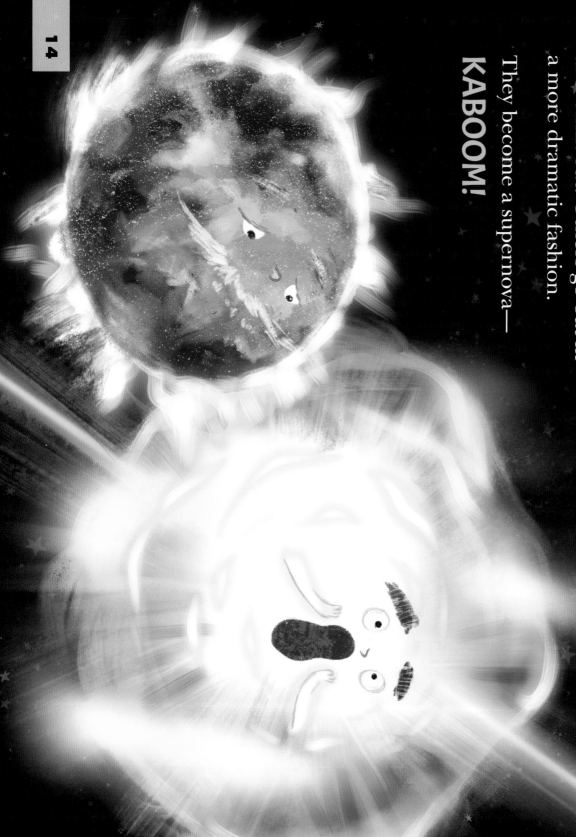

In old age, all my stars start to run out of energy. Sadly, they begin to die.

They e x p a n d .
They glow red.

Some of these red giants die quietly—after a long time, they just cool and blink out. Others go out in a more dramatic fashion.

They become a supernova—
KABOOM!

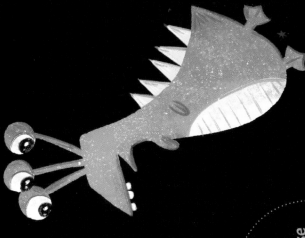

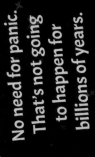

Oh no! Should we tell those Earthlings that their sun is going to die, too?

No need for panic. That's not going to happen for billions of years.

Even without the drama, Earthlings love to watch the stars. Someone even wrote a song about my twinkling stars.

But I'm going to let you in on a little secret—they aren't really twinkling. They shine with the same brightness all the time.

They only look like they are twinkling because of Earth's atmosphere. As the starlight passes through the atmosphere, *it bends.*

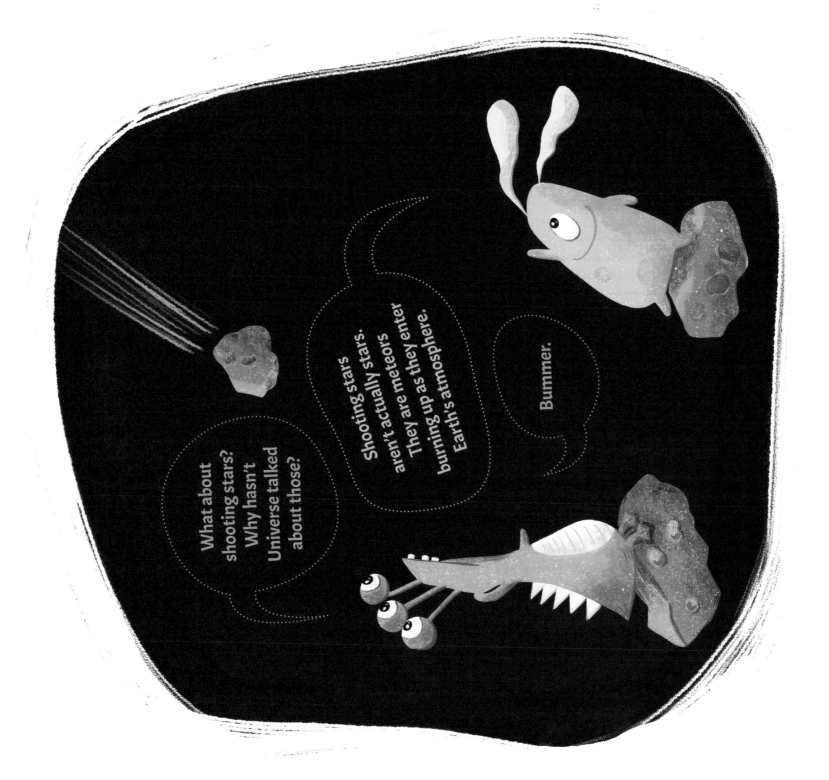

Earthlings have looked up to my stars in the night sky since ancient times. They saw all kinds of pictures in the stars—like a giant, cosmic dot-to-dot.

Constellations!

Some constellations are named after figures from myths.

Others are named after animals. Ancient Earthlings used these pictures to tell stories.

Um, that doesn't look like a bear.

Use your imagination!

Ancient Earthlings also made a map of the night sky with those constellations as guides.

Why would you need that, you ask?
After all, you aren't flying around space
(well, sometimes you are, nowadays).

People used
those maps
for navigation.
Imagine being on
a dark stretch of
land or sea.
How do you
know where
you're going?

**Follow the stars,
of course!**

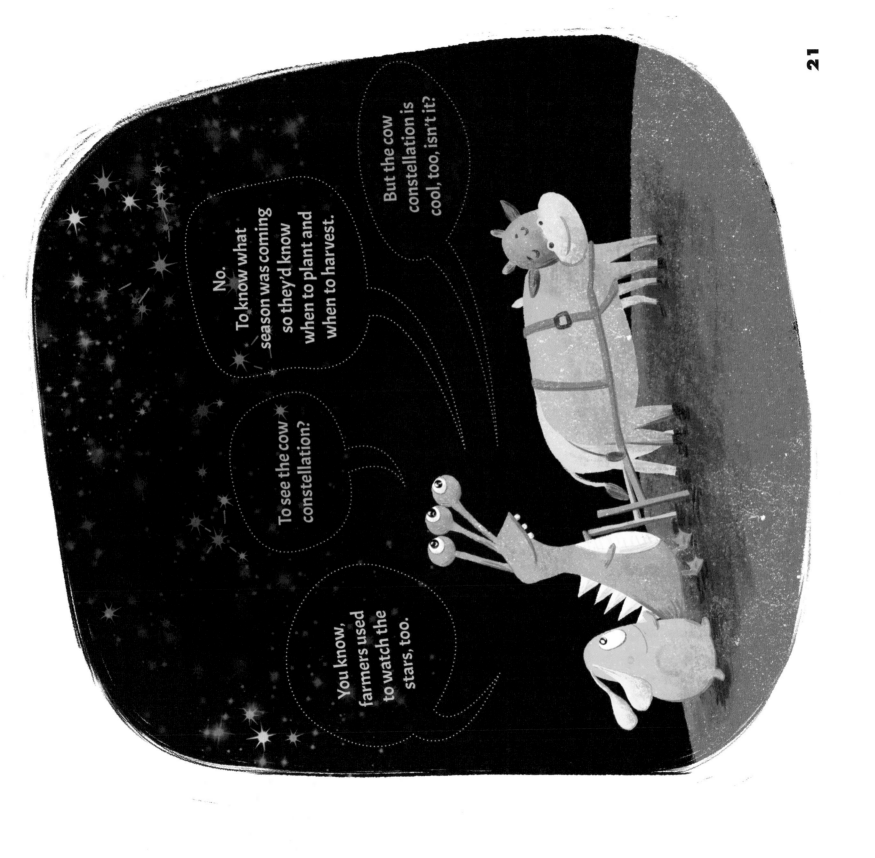

However, using the stars to navigate is a bit tricky because your planet is *spinning*, *orbiting*, and *tilting*.

Because of all your planetary acrobatics, you see different stars in different months throughout the year. The stars you see also depend on where you are on the planet.

Luckily, you Earthlings are pretty smart!

But . . . many of you don't look up at the stars like you used to.

You don't tell as many stories.
Or use the stars for navigation.
Or wonder.
You have your own lights now.
And technology.

All of that is making my magnificent treasures hard to see. It's as though the stars are shy and hiding.

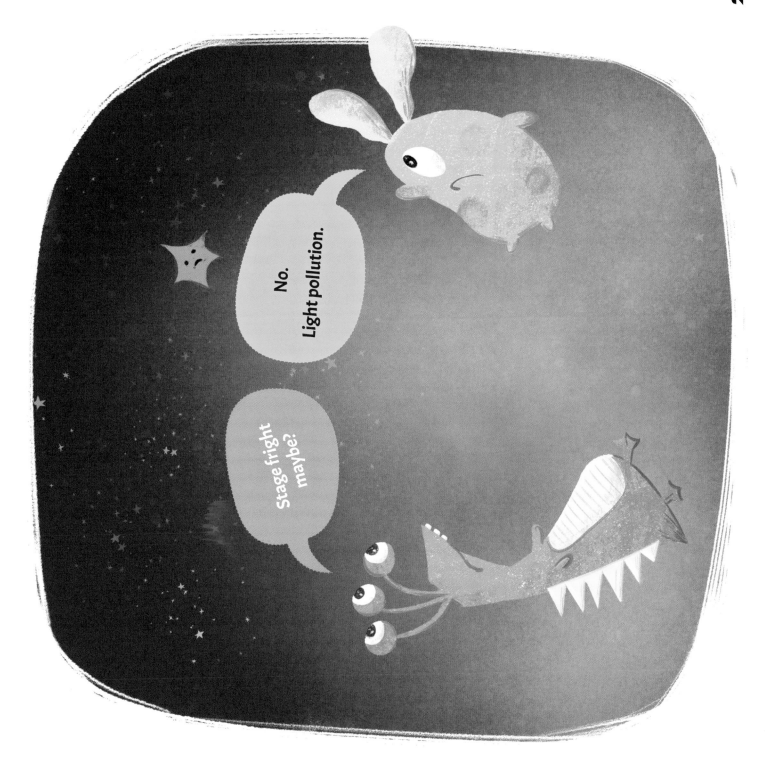

So, turn off a light.

Or two.

Find a dark sky.
Marvel at the wonder of stars.

"**Star light**, star bright . . . . ."
And wish upon a star.

Get to Know the Constellations

There are dozens of constellations in the night sky. Some of them are very recognizable once you learn what they look like.

A white dwarf star

credit: NASA/JPL-Caltech

WHAT YOU NEED

sidewalk chalk, somewhere to draw, 10–20 small rocks, information (and pictures) about constellations

WHAT YOU DO

Begin with research about constellations. Find one you like and learn the story behind it.

Take a picture of your constellation outside with you. On the ground, position your rocks as though they were the stars in your constellation. Use the chalk to connect the stars so you have a sidewalk constellation. Label it.

Once you know a few constellations, go outside on a clear night. Can you find your constellation? Was it easier or harder than you thought it might be? You may want to record where you see your constellation in the sky at different times and in different seasons.

Team up with a friend or family member and share your constellations. You can tell the stories behind them.

Glossary

atmosphere: a blanket of gases around the earth.

constellation: a group of stars that form a picture.

galaxy: a collection of star systems held together by gravity.

gravity: a force that pulls objects toward each other and all objects to the earth.

light pollution: too much manmade light during the night, so that it is hard to see stars.

light year: the distance that light travels in one year, equal to about 5.88 trillion miles.

meteor: a rock or chunk of ice that falls toward Earth from space and shows up as a bright streak in the sky.

Milky Way: the galaxy that contains our solar system.

navigate: to find your way from one place to another.

orbit: the path of an object circling another in space.

planet: a large body in space that orbits the sun and does not produce its own light. There are eight planets.

protostar: a new star.

solar system: a family of eight planets and their moons that orbit the sun.

solitary: alone.

star: an astronomical body that makes its own light.

supernova: an exploding star at the end of its life.

technology: the use of science to invent things or solve problems.

vast: huge.

universe: everything that exists, everywhere.

The Horsehead Nebula

credit: NASA

Orion

The Milky Way

EXPLORE AWESOME ADAPTATIONS IN THIS PICTURE BOOK SCIENCE SET!

Check out more titles at www.nomadpress.net

Nomad Press

A division of Nomad Communications

10 9 8 7 6 5 4 3 2 1

This book was manufactured by CGB Printers,
North Mankato, Minnesota, United States
March 2021, Job #1018009

ISBN Softcover: 978-1-61930-992-0
ISBN Hardcover: 978-1-61930-989-0

Educational Consultant, Marla Conn

Questions regarding the ordering of this book should be addressed to
Nomad Press
2456 Christian St., White River Junction, VT 05001
www.nomadpress.net

Printed in the United States.